T0169572

We Gather at This Table

We Gather at This Table

Anna V. Ostenso Moore
Illustrations by Peter Krueger

CHURCH
PUBLISHING
INCORPORATED

Copyright © 2020 by Anna V. Ostenso Moore
Illustrations copyright © 2020 by Peter Krueger

All rights reserved. No part of this book may be reproduced, stored in a retrieval
system, or transmitted in any form or by any means, electronic or mechanical,
including photocopying, recording, or otherwise, without the written permission
of the publisher.

Church Publishing
19 East 34th Street
New York, NY 10016
www.churchpublishing.org

Cover design and typeset by: Beth Oberholtzer

A record of this book is available from the Library of Congress.

ISBN -13: 9781640652521 (Hardcover)
ISBN -13: 9781640652538 (ebook)

To Navy Jane, Wallace Carl, and Wrigley Brian
with love and wonder
—Anna

To Amy Jensen, Carol Jensen,
and Molly Schaaf
—Peter

Presented to

_____

From

_____

On the occasion of

_____

Date

_____

Beloved Child of God,

We gather at this table
with family, strangers, friends, and neighbors,

with prayer, Sacred Stories, songs, peace, and our gifts,

with joy, doubt, questions, wonder—
all of ourselves.

we gather to share this bread and wine.

We bless this bread
as Jesus did, spending one last night with friends—
eating, teaching, celebrating, remembering.

We break this bread
to remember
God with us, seen and unseen:

Creator creating and loving,

Jesus holding, healing,
praying, proclaiming, defying,

We eat this bread
to hope for a holy moment of
harmony and unity
in the brokenness of our humanity.

We drink this wine
to share the Sacred Story,
to embrace holy mystery
together—to be the Church,
followers of Jesus.

We share this meal
at the altar, Jesus's table,

so that we may share it at our tables,

in friends' homes,

in the world,
wherever we are.

We gather at this table
to know that God is here.

Family Pages

Use this page to share where you notice God.

A Note from the Author

Dear Families,

For thousands of years, followers of the way of Jesus have gathered and shared bread and wine. Like us, in ritual they sought to be near God and join in the Sacred Story of God incarnate, God here on earth. Rituals around the bread and wine have changed, adapting to the gifts and resources of individual faith communities, the local culture, and understandings of God. Although we call it by different names: Holy Eucharist, Mass, Communion, and some use wine and some use grape juice, we all share this holy meal as an outward and visible sign of an inward and spiritual grace: a sacrament. Although we approach the altar for a variety of reasons, we enter with our whole selves into this great mystery. We enter as individual parts of the body of Christ, unique children of God joined together in this ritual.

As I wrote this book, I thought of the children I love: my nieces, nephews, godchildren, and the children who run through my faith community. I deeply desire to share with our youngest generations (and with all generations) the transformative power of the bread and wine. I suspect this is a desire in most of you who have important children in your life.

Yet we know that God and Holy Eucharist cannot be contained by our understanding or fully explained with words. And we do not always know what is going on inside of ourselves when we worship. The good news is that we do not need to have all of the answers. We need to start with our own voice and reasons for why we are fed by Eucharist. Though our personal thoughts about what this holy meal means might change over time (or even week to week), we each have a valuable voice and holy wisdom to offer.

This book was written to provide a tool for families to explore what sharing the bread and wine means for them and how it inspires their lives. On the following pages, I have suggested ways to help you and your child engage in worship. Children have a concept of God and a sense of the Holy that changes as they age. They naturally embrace awe, wonder, and mystery. Children give us adults the gift of renewing our own imagination and sense of mystery that can dull over the years. We need to respect their experiences while helping them find the vocabulary and practices to sense, name, question, and wonder about God. One of the best places to start is within our own faith community.

With peace from my family to yours,
Anna V. Ostenso Moore

Worship Engagement Suggestions

These suggestions are meant as starting points to be adapted and personalized. You know your child/children. You know your faith community.

Remember that you are enough.

As caregivers, we want to share our faith with children. Yet finding the words sometimes seems so hard. We can be shut down by voices of doubt saying things like, "Don't mess this up!"

You, like them, are beloved children of God. You are enough. Your children do not need an expert. They need someone who loves them and who is willing to share their faith with them, engage their questions, and encourage them.

Have age-appropriate expectations.

We arrive at worship in a variety of moods week to week; so do children. Likewise, some parts of worship will speak to us more than others, as they will to children.

Each developmental stage of children brings joys and challenges. There will be moments when your child is fully engaged in a part of the worship, like the passing of the peace. Encourage and rejoice in these moments. There will be times when your child only seems to want to scream (and you may too). Take a break for a few minutes from worship and remember that this stage is not forever. This too will pass.

When they are young, bring soft toys or other items to help them be present. As they age, experiment with other tools of engagement, like colored pencils for the bulletin.

Show how you worship.

Children learn from what they experience and observe. They recognize your reverence from your body language and they will naturally begin to imitate you. Encourage this. Hold hands during parts of the service like the Lord's Prayer to reinforce the connection of that moment. From the actions of the whole community, children see that Holy Eucharist is something special. Even without knowing the "why," your child will feel welcomed, accepted, and beloved in their community and in the eyes of God.

Share your words.

We all have our own reasons for sharing the bread and wine with others. Share yours: Why do you worship? Where do you notice God showing up?

Faith communities speak a language particular to themselves and the larger Church. You are one of their translators. Share that vocabulary. Define or explain what children may hear or notice.

Encourage wonder and curiosity.

Let your child choose where to sit. Sometimes this may mean a couple of different spots during worship. Or, if it is a special occasion like baptism, encourage your child to find spaces where they can engage to the best of their ability, especially considering sight lines. Follow their eyes, notice what catches their attention, and wonder with them.

Our spaces and what worship leaders wear tell our Sacred Stories. At appropriate times, wonder with your child about what they notice. Allow your child to step into the pulpit, touch the water in the font, or sit near the organist during the postlude.

Expand your community.

Worship includes proclaiming your beliefs with others. Offer a friendly smile to others sitting with children. Introduce yourself and your child to those who sit by them and those who they see leading worship. Remind them that their godparents and/or other important adults are people who have committed to supporting their faith life.

When you have questions, ask your own spiritual leaders. Not only will you learn, you will model for your children that it is okay to say, "I don't know. Let's find out."

Visit other worshipping communities. Notice their similarities and differences from your own community. Respectfully, teach the reasons for the differences.

Have fun.

Read Sacred Stories

Together, look up in the Bible some of the Sacred Stories that inspired this book's illustrations:

We bless this bread as Jesus did	Luke 22:15–20
	Ecclesiastes 2:24–25
Jesus holding, healing, praying, proclaiming, defying	Mark 8:22–26
	John 8:2–11
	Mark 8:1–8
	Matthew 4:1–4
Holy Spirit dancing in our midst	Acts 2:2–13
	2 Samuel 6:14–19

Find the illustration in this book that accompanies the biblical story you are listening to or reading. With a playful spirit, wonder about it together as a family. Wonder what part is most important to you. Wonder what stories you would include. Wonder about the differences of answers. Do not assess each other's answers as right or wrong. Instead hold up each response as holy.